Nudes of Yesteryear/Eros Books/New York

To order
additional copies of
Nudes of Yesteryear,
send $15.00 per copy
to: Eros Books
110 West 40th Street,
New York, N. Y. 10018.

If you wish
to learn about other
books published by
Eros Books,
simply send
a postal card
with your name
and address
and the words
"Mailing List"
to: Eros Books,
110 West 40th Street,
New York, N. Y. 10018.

DESIGNED BY HERB LUBALIN.

NUDES OF YESTERYEAR

LIBRARY OF CONGRESS NUMBER:
63-18409.

PRINTED IN THE
UNITED STATES OF AMERICA.

CREDIT, AND THANKS,
TO HENRY LENOIR
OF THE VESUVIO CAFE
IN SAN FRANCISCO FOR
PHOTOGRAPHS ON PAGES
28-29, 50-51, 67, 70, 76.

Admirers of the female form, connoisseurs of the photographic art, and collectors of Gay Nineties memorabilia will be delighted to see this book in print. Those who worked tenaciously and lovingly to produce it—the staff of the award-winning (and now suppressed) quarterly Eros—are not only delighted but relieved that it is finally appearing.

Originally intended as a feature for Eros, this collection of antique photographs just grew and grew until, after several years, it became large enough to constitute this book.

To locate the ladies in Nudes of Yesteryear, Eros researchers hunted through archives, attics, book-stalls, and family trunks all over Europe and America. The resulting portfolio depicts French girls in the dingy, drafty ateliers of fin de siècle Paris (many of them are the models who posed for Toulouse-Lautrec, Renoir, and other celebrated artists of the period); voluptuous Italian girls in the studios of Florence; and carefree American girls pausing on the Grand Tour of Europe to strike poses that they would never have dreamed of assuming back home.

Unfortunately, the issue of Eros in which the choicest of these lovely nudes were to appear was banned by censors of the United States Post Office. Sadly, the pictures were put aside. But the editors could not forget them and plans for a full-length book slowly began to take shape. Now, more than two years after their suppression, these mementos of a quaint and vaguely scandalous past are finally seeing the light of print. Sensuous, naughty, provocative, at times endearingly funny, these nudes of yesteryear could not remain hidden forever.

They are as irrepressible as the erotic impulse itself.

Lydia
24

194

206
J. MANDEL

SAPI
2669

62

140

116

3952/1

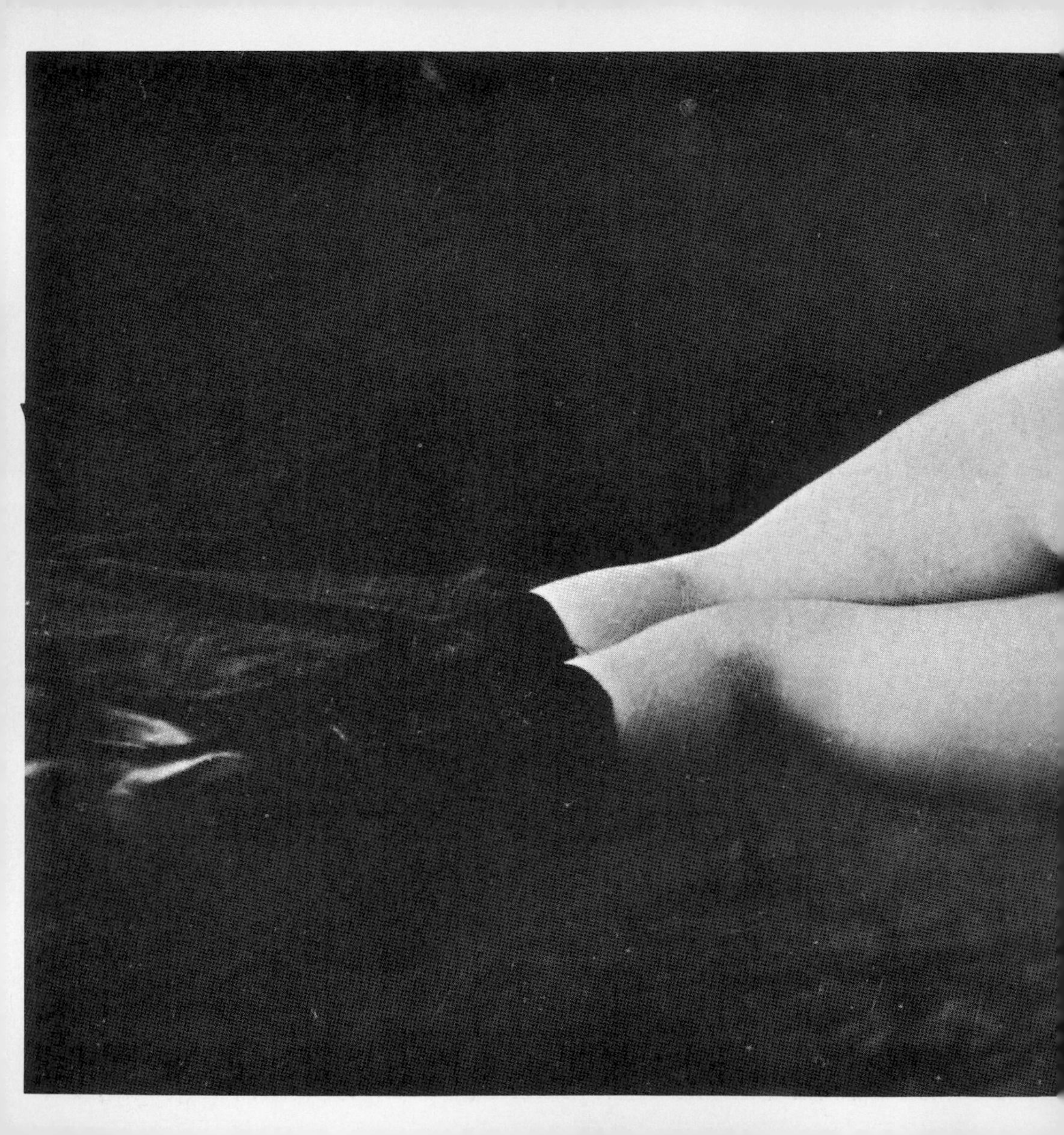

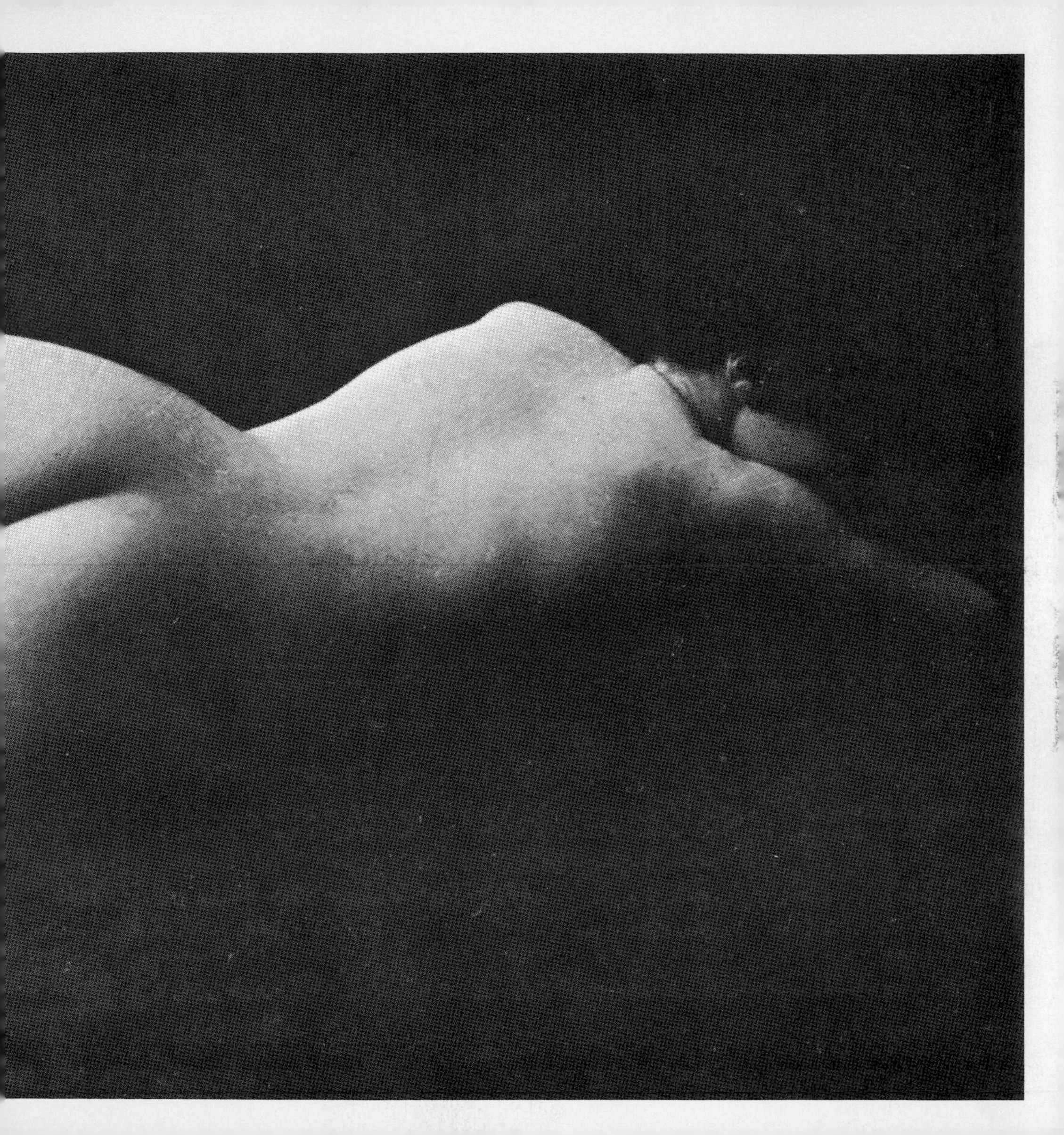

Super
1125

REGIST

COMP. IND. FOT
PROP. ART. REGIST.-1923
78

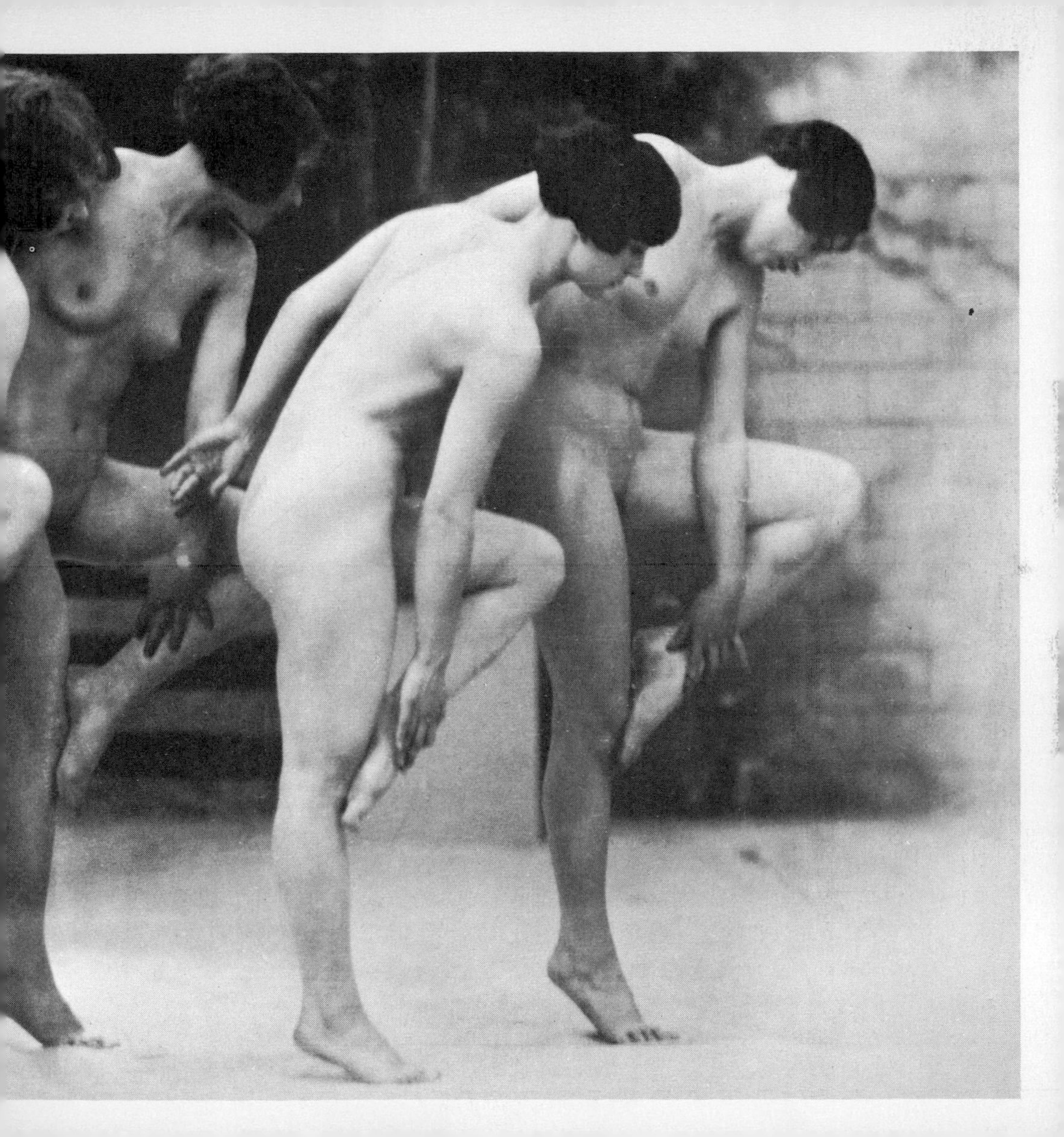

139

3945/5

E.L.F.
Paris
12

E.L.F.

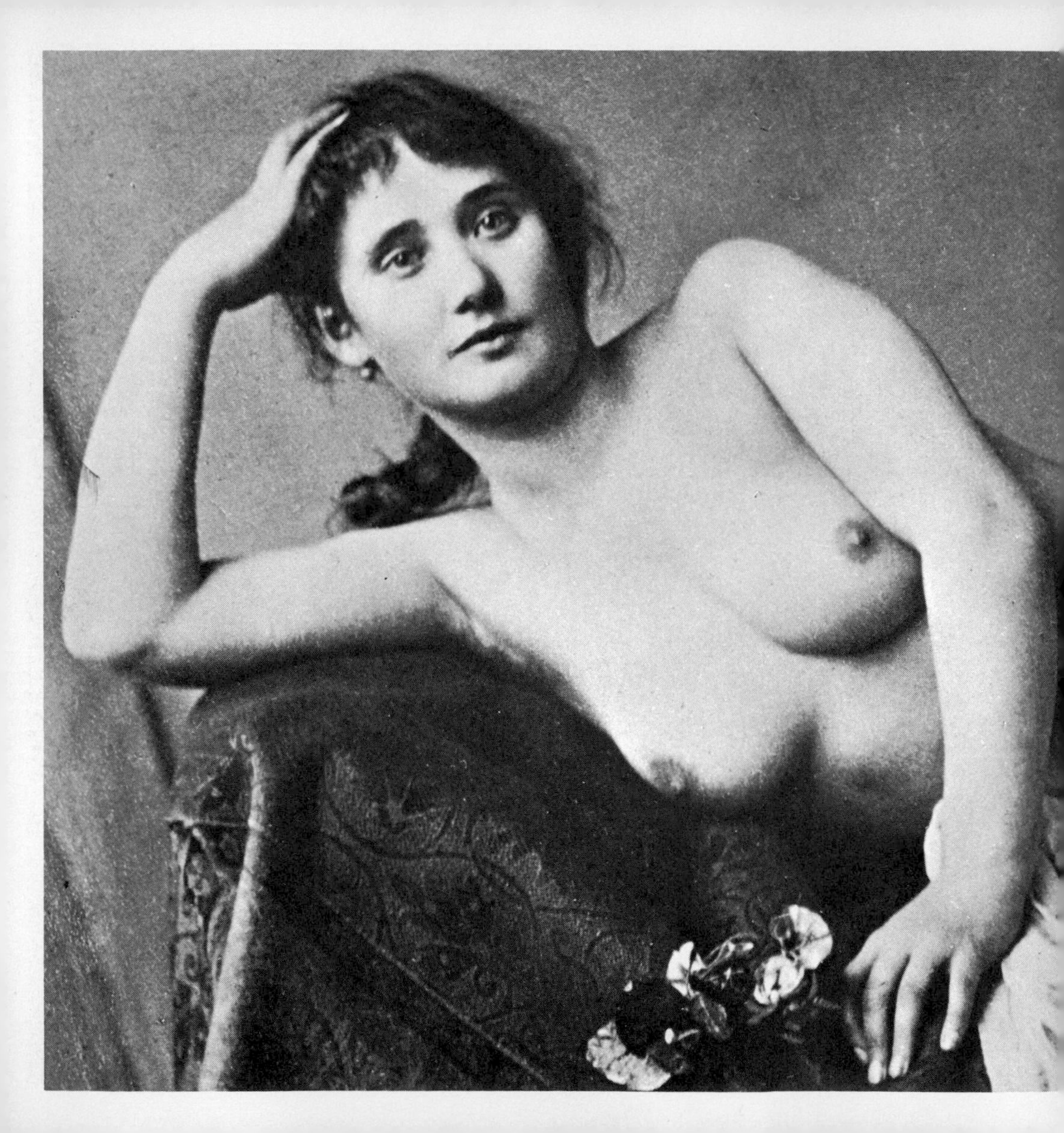

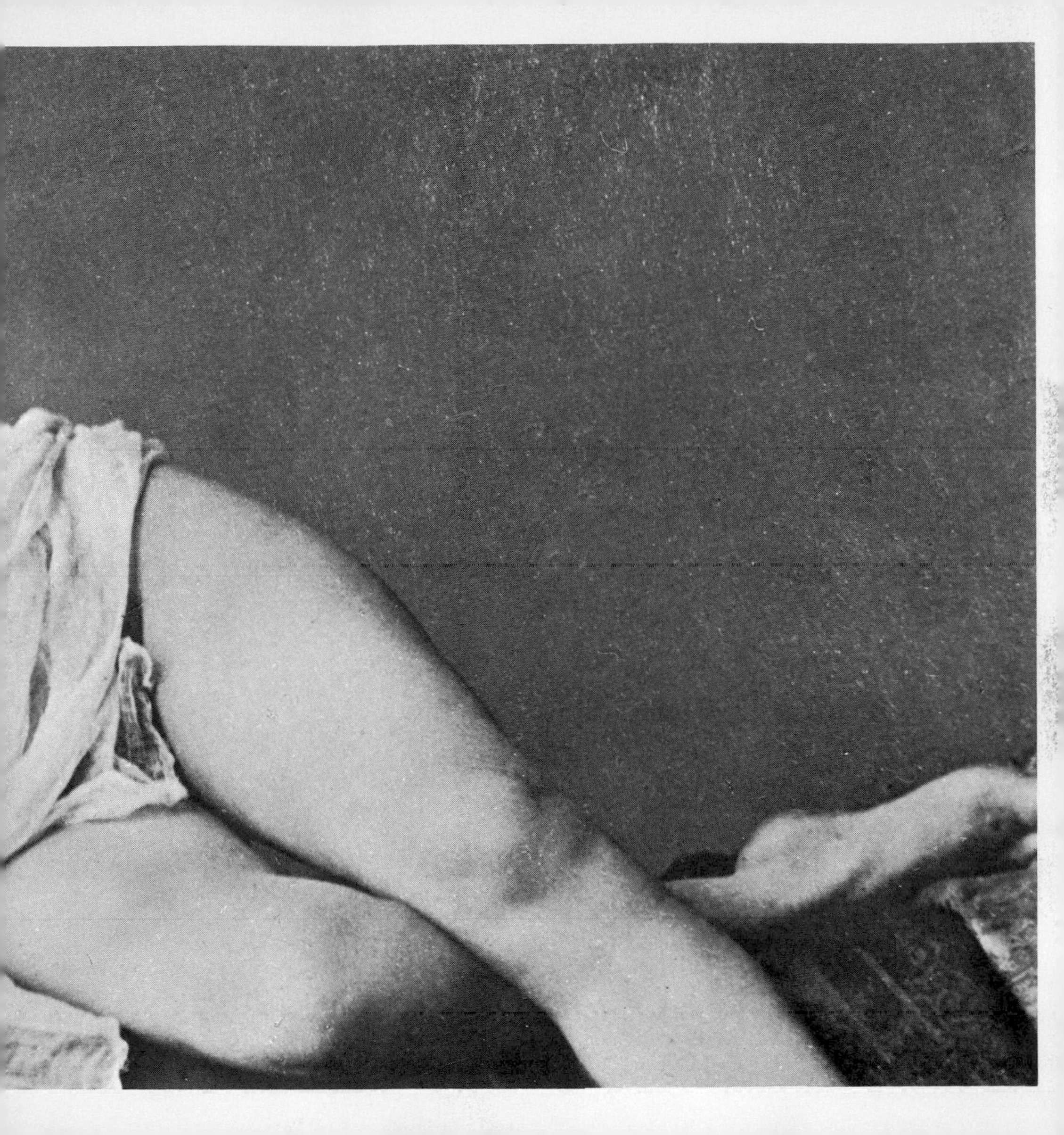

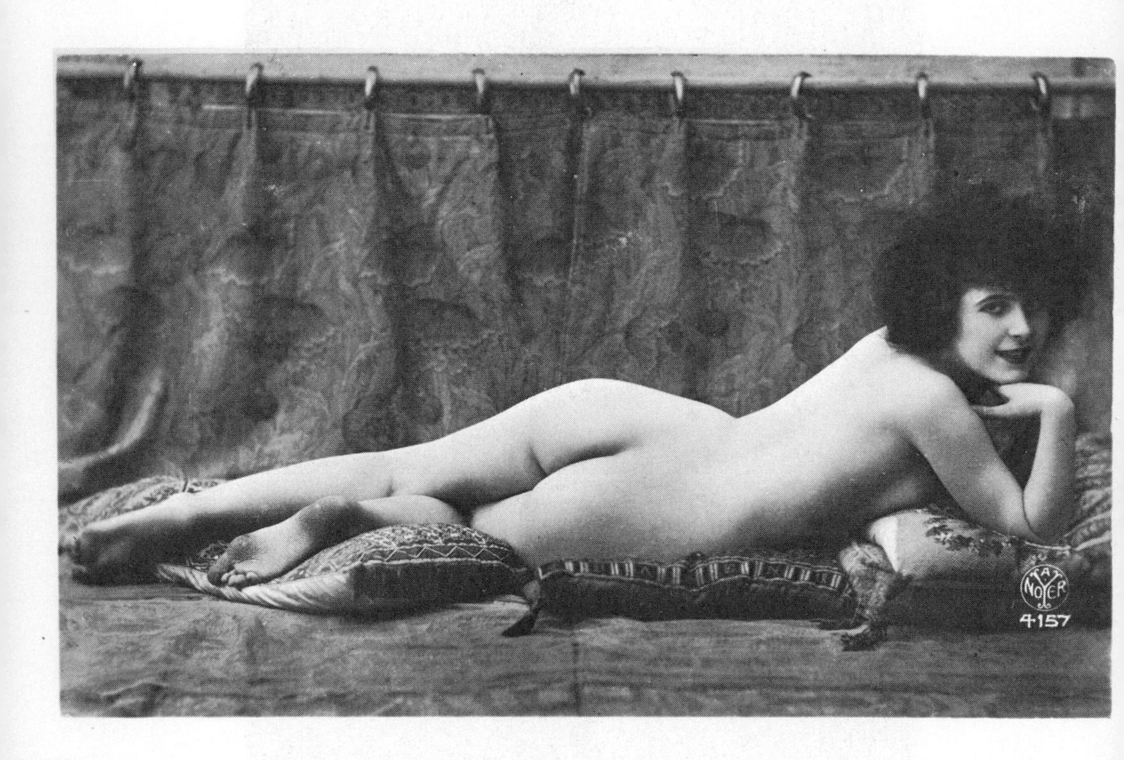
NOYER
4157

S·A·P·I·
2404

621/9.
© ALTA

SERIE 2A
PARIS

P.C
PARIS
1222

P.C
PARIS
1757

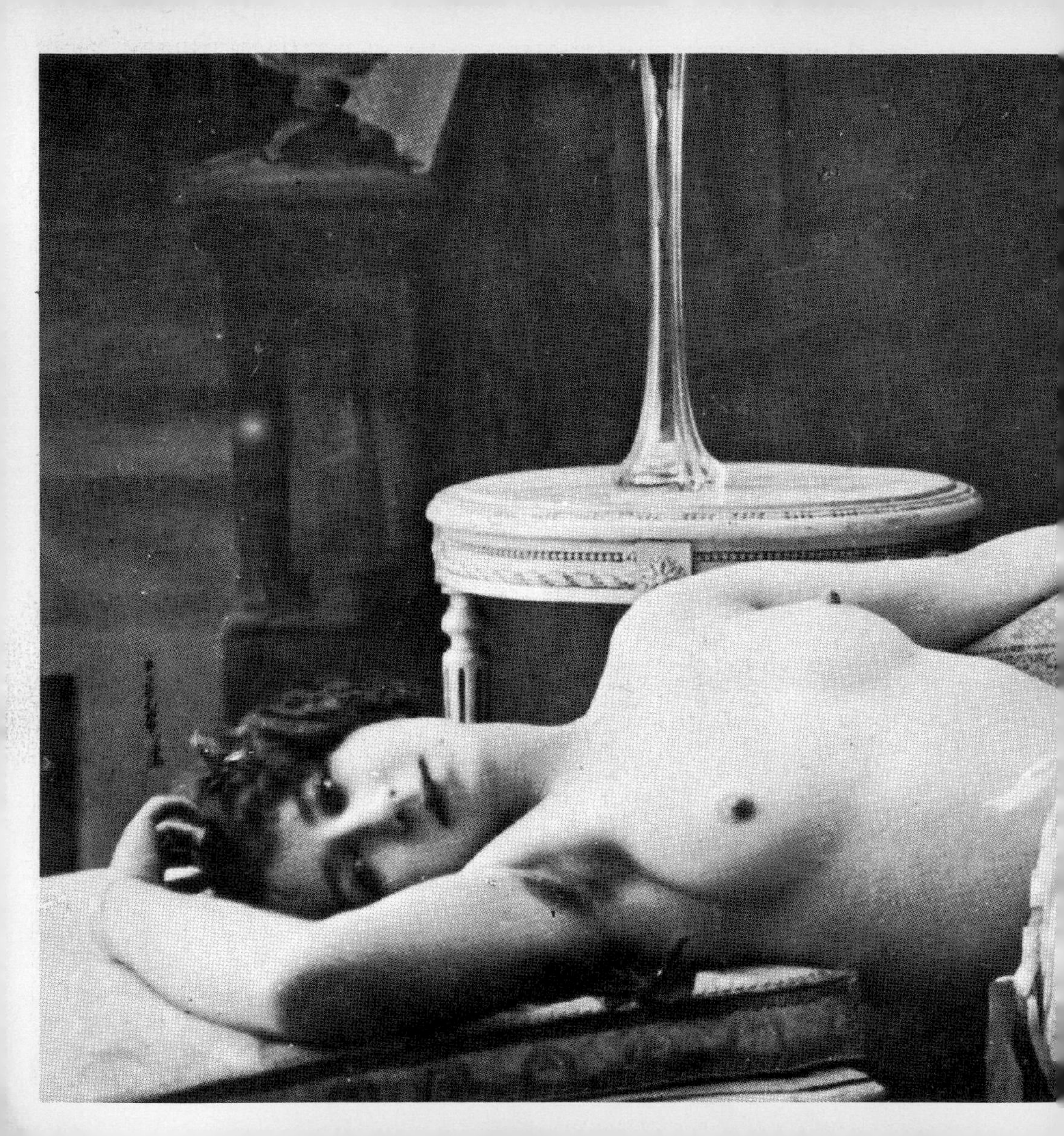

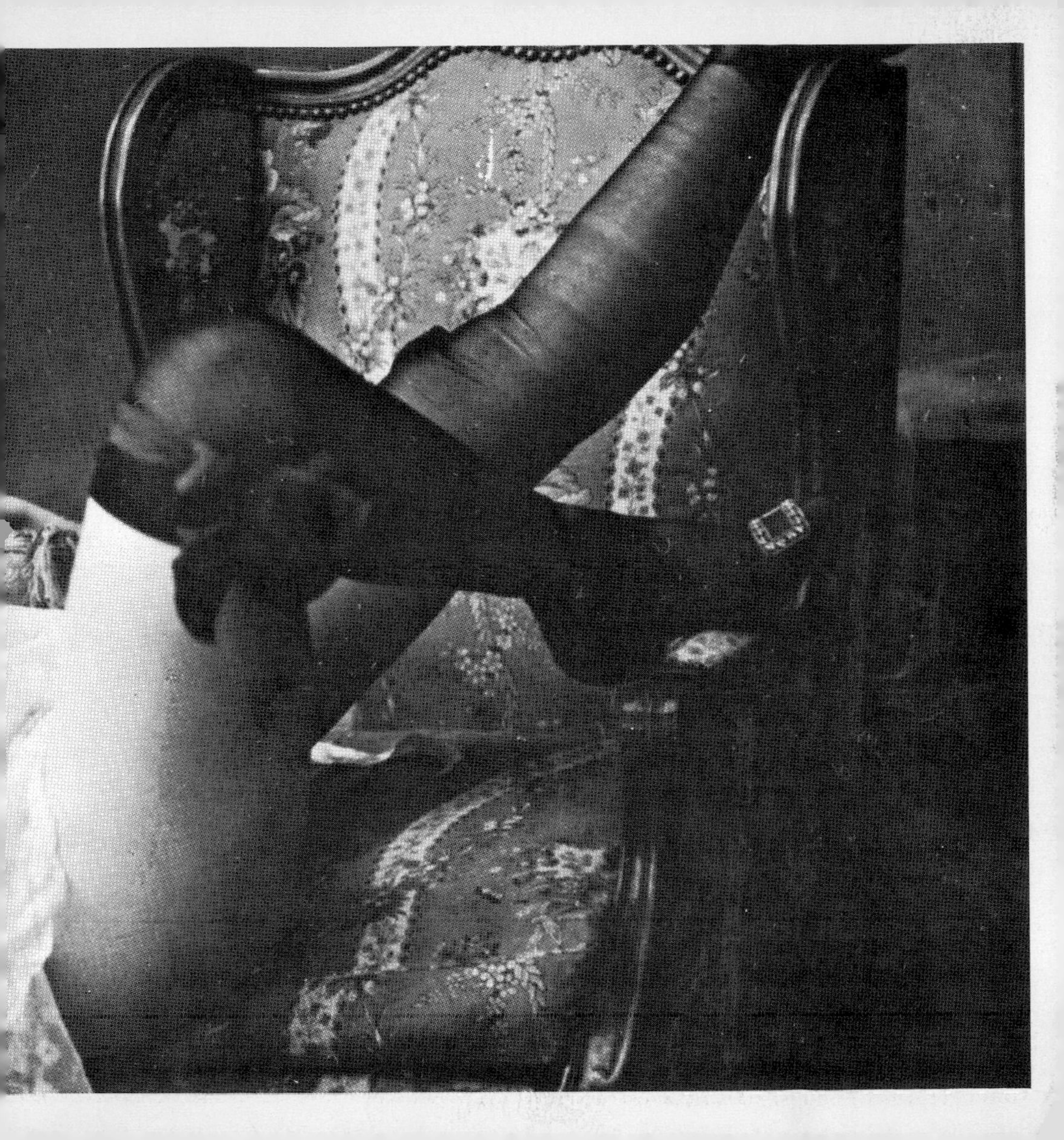

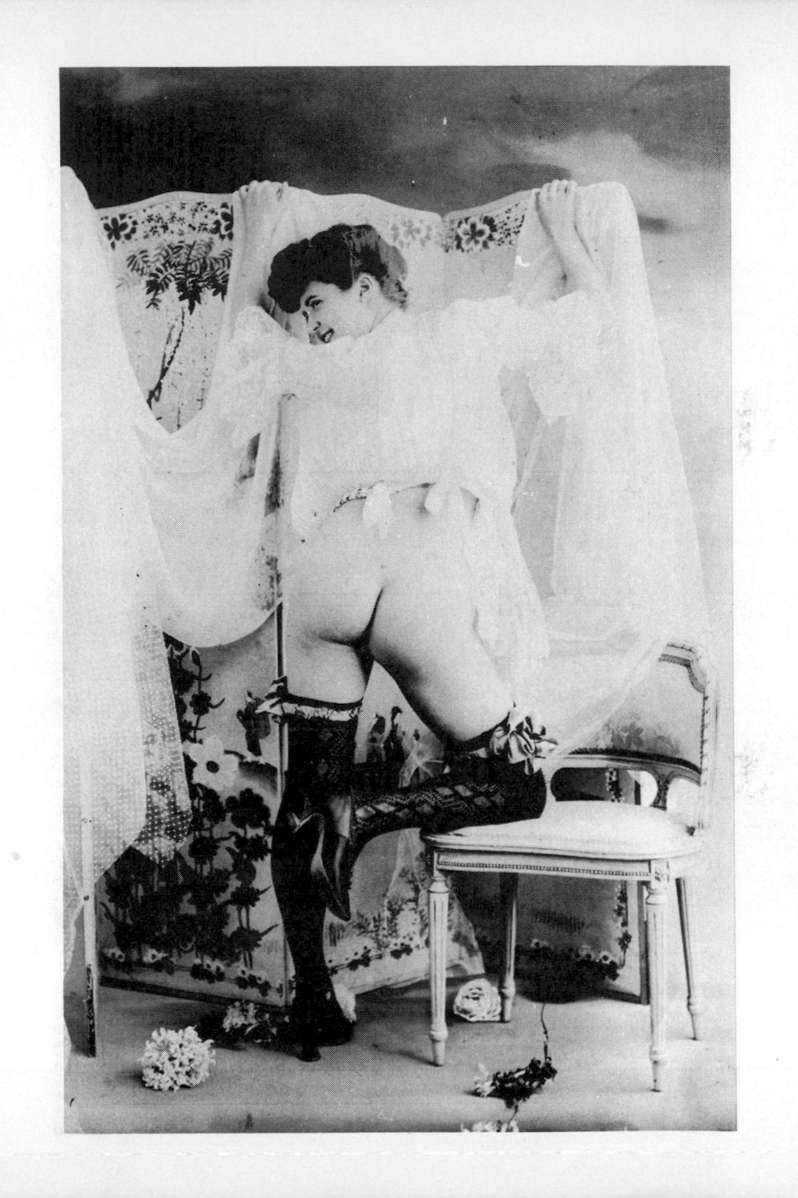

SAPI
2389

J. J. - 8720. - AIX-les-BAINS.

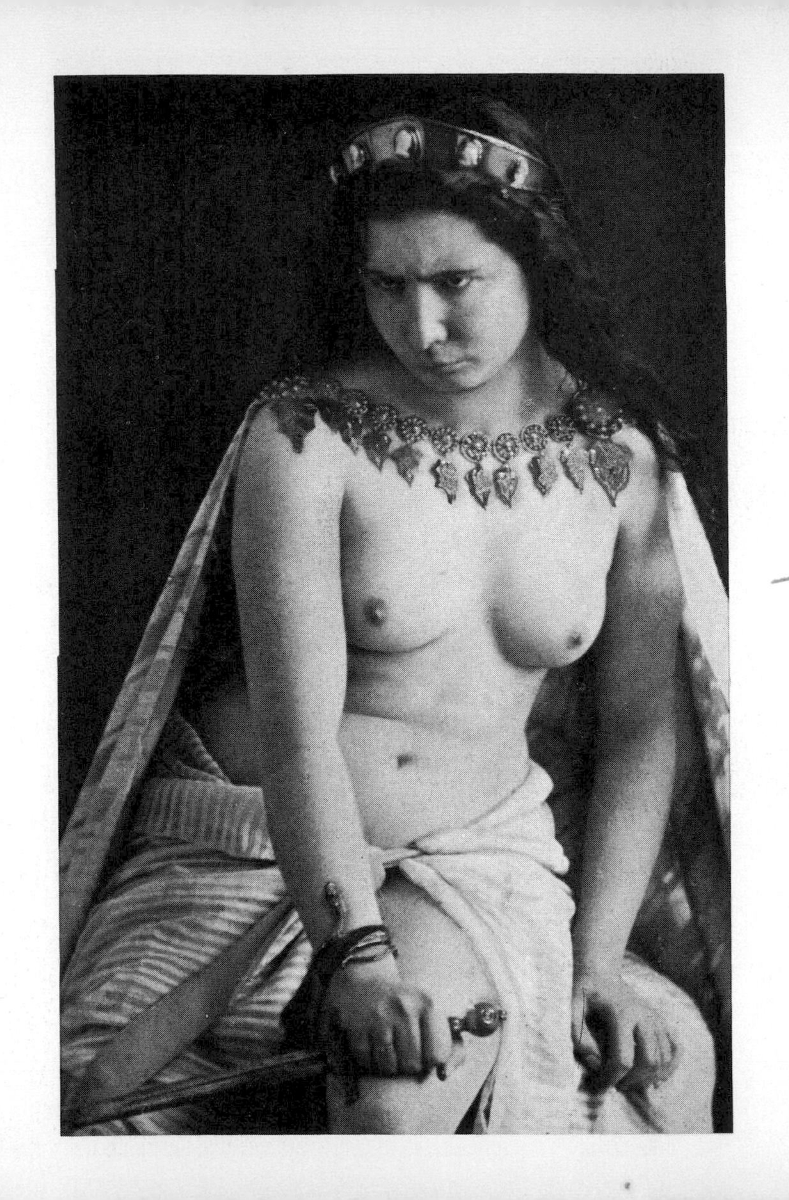

157

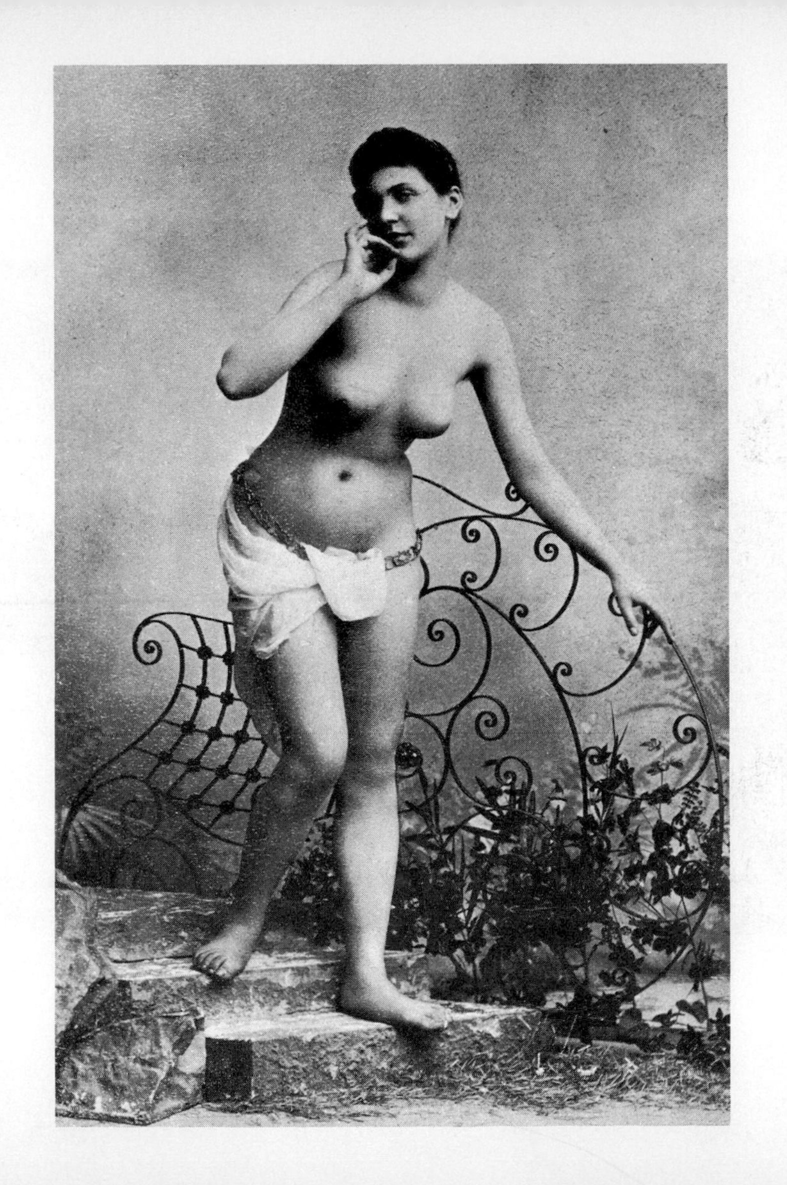

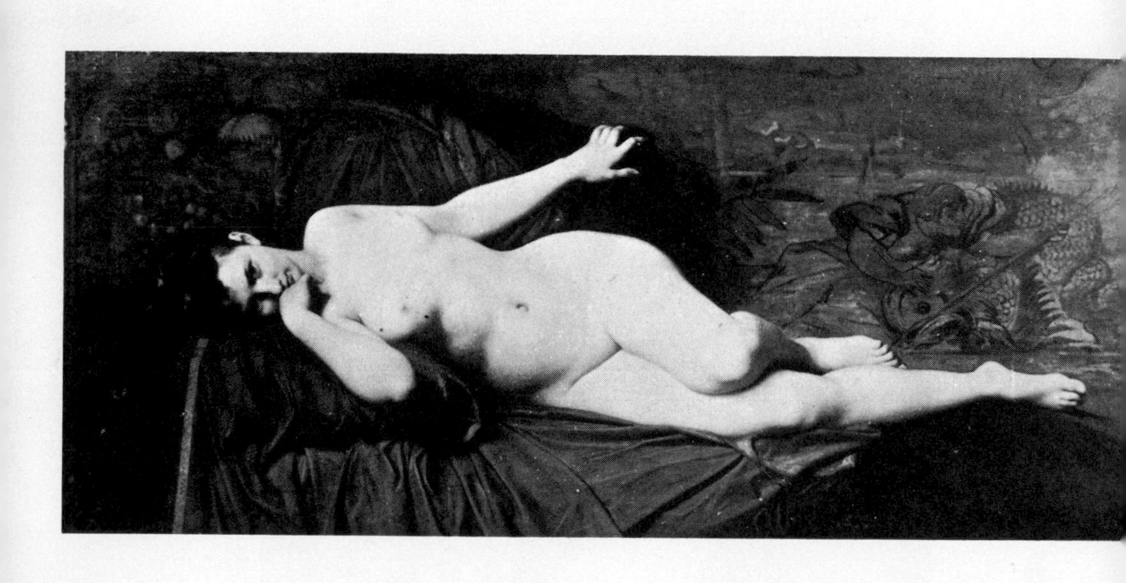

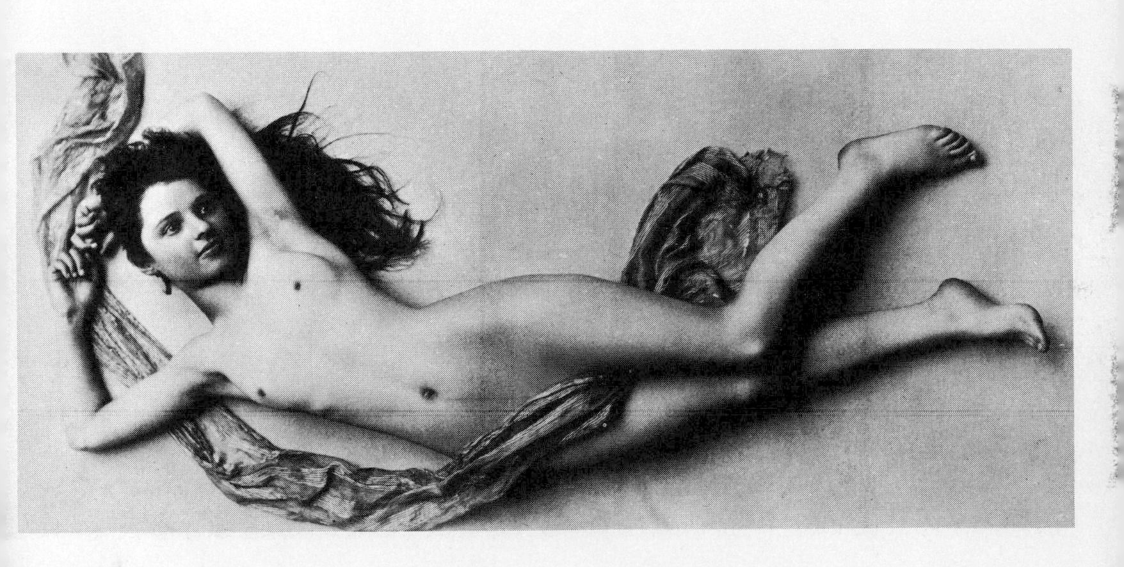

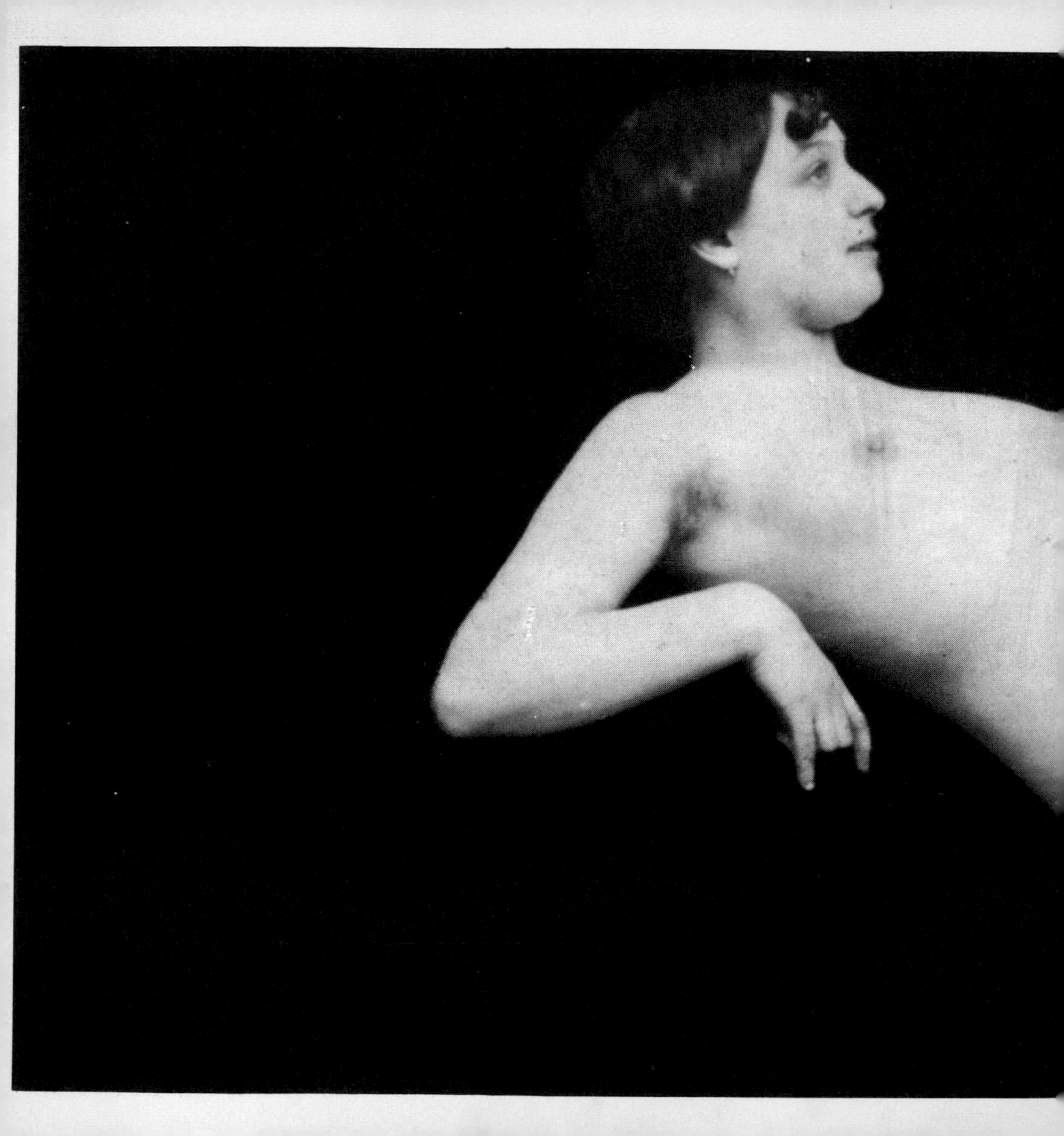

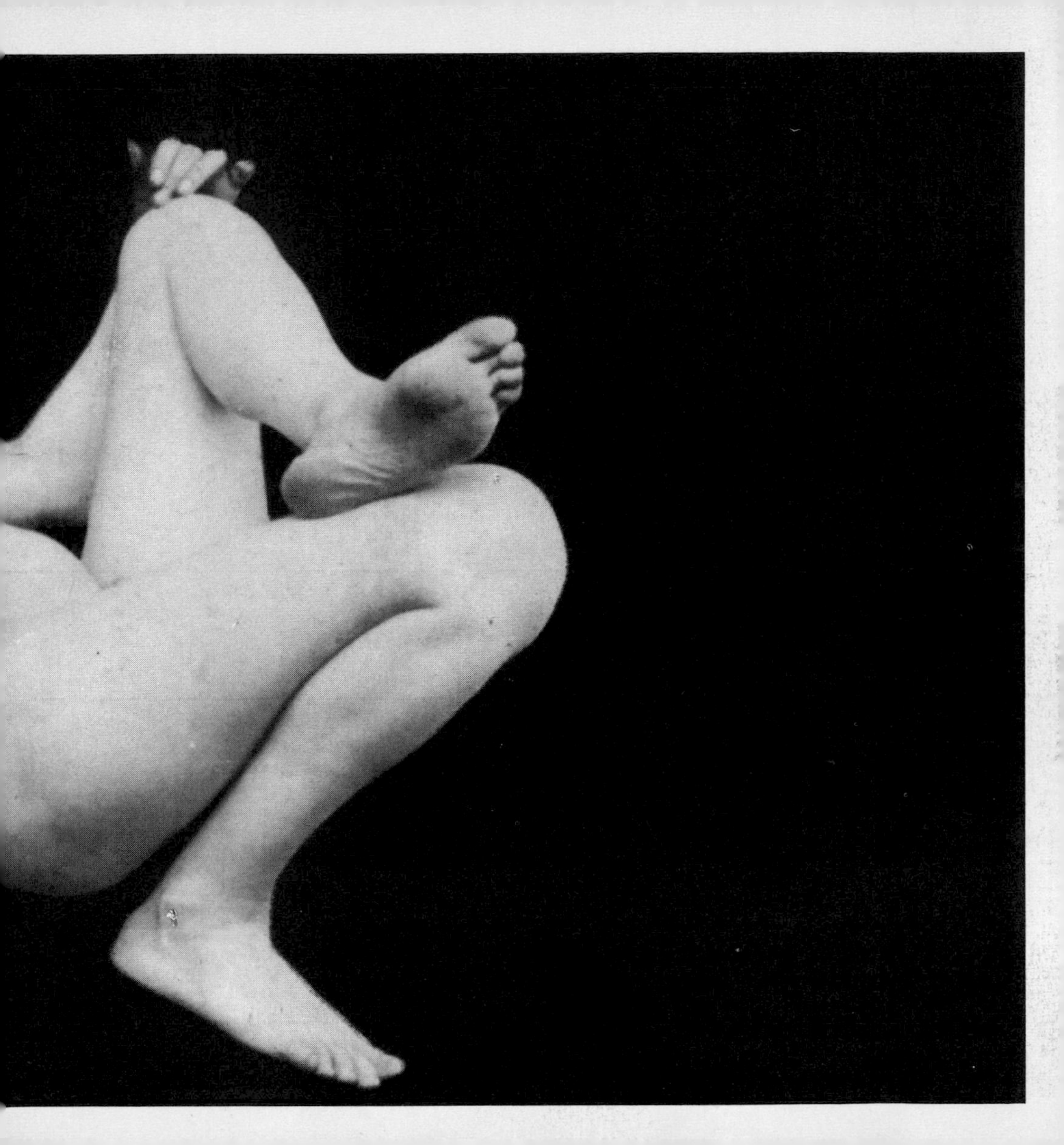

82